AWESOME FRUITS COLORING BOOK FOR KIDS

VOLUME ONE

Copyright ©2023 by **3G SOLUTIONS LLC**

All rights reserved. No portion of this publication may be reproduced, stored in a retrieval system, or transmitted in any form or by any means – electronic, mechanical, photocopying, recording, scanning, or otherwise, without the prior written permission of the publisher.

INTRODUCTION

This captivating book is designed for children and brims with delightful illustrations of various fruits, each corresponding to a letter of the English alphabet. While showcasing familiar fruits, it also introduces youngsters to some lesser-known varieties, presenting an opportunity for them to explore different fruit categories.

Within these pages, each fruit illustration is accompanied by two distinct skeleton designs awaiting the imaginative touch of young artists. The first design invites children to apply their preferred colors directly, while the second provides a playful outline for creative embellishments. Additionally, an empty third page awaits, inviting children to craft their very own fruit designs for each letter of the alphabet.

As a special bonus, the book concludes with a dedicated page where children can meticulously document the array of colors they've employed to bring the illustrated fruits to life. This interactive and educational journey encourages both artistic expression and fruit discovery, making it an ideal companion for curious young minds.

THESE FRUITS REPRESENT EACH ALPHABETS

 APPLE	 BANANA	 CANTALOUPE	 DATE	 EGGPLANT
 FIG	 GOOSEBERRY	 HONEYDEW	 ITA PALM	 JUJUBE
 KIWI	 LEMON	 MANGO	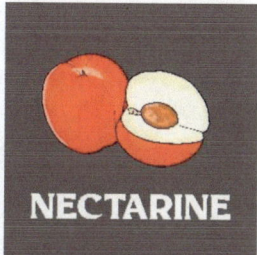 NECTARINE	 OLIVE
 PAPAYA	 QUINCE	 RAMBUTAN	 STAR FRUIT	 TANGELO
 UGLI	 VOAVANGA	 WATERMELON	 XIGUA	 YUMBERRY
 ZUCHINNI				

AWESOME FRUITS
COLORING BOOK FOR KIDS
VOLUME 1

BELONGS

TO

....

....

....

APPLE

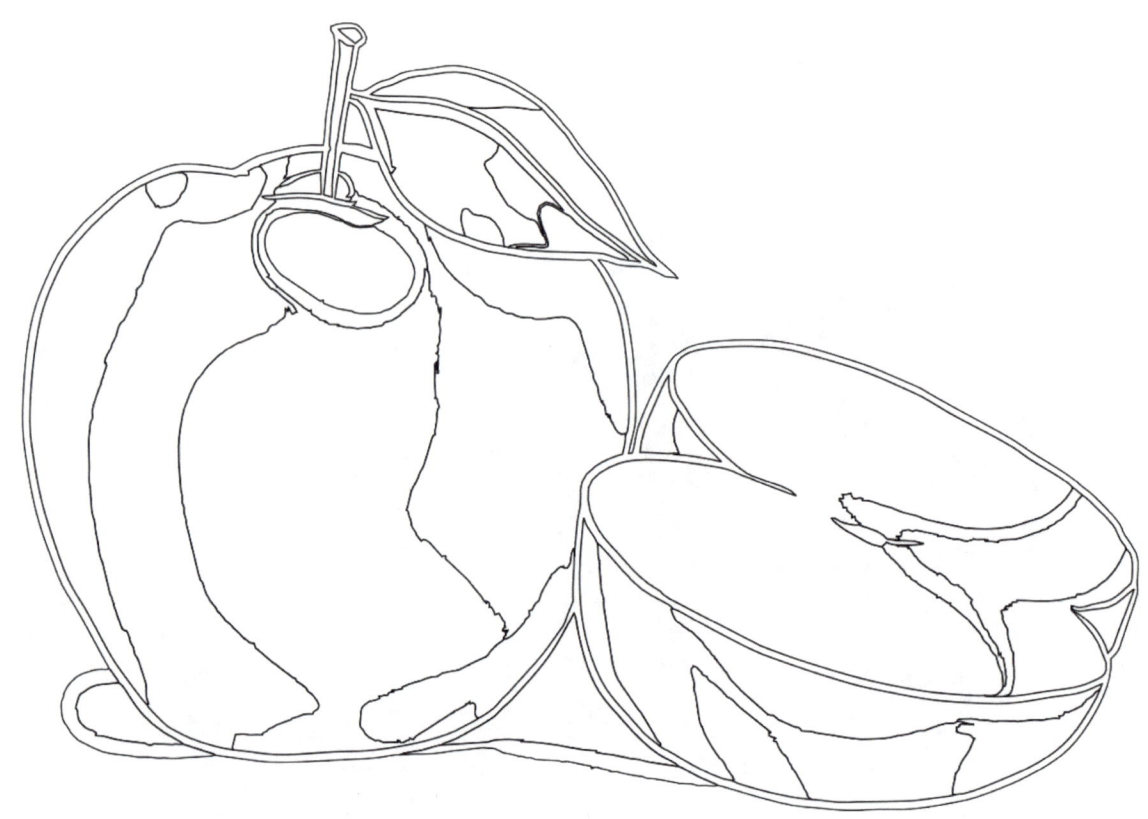

APPLE

APPLE

ILLUSTRATE YOUR OWN APPLE ON THIS CANVAS

BANANA

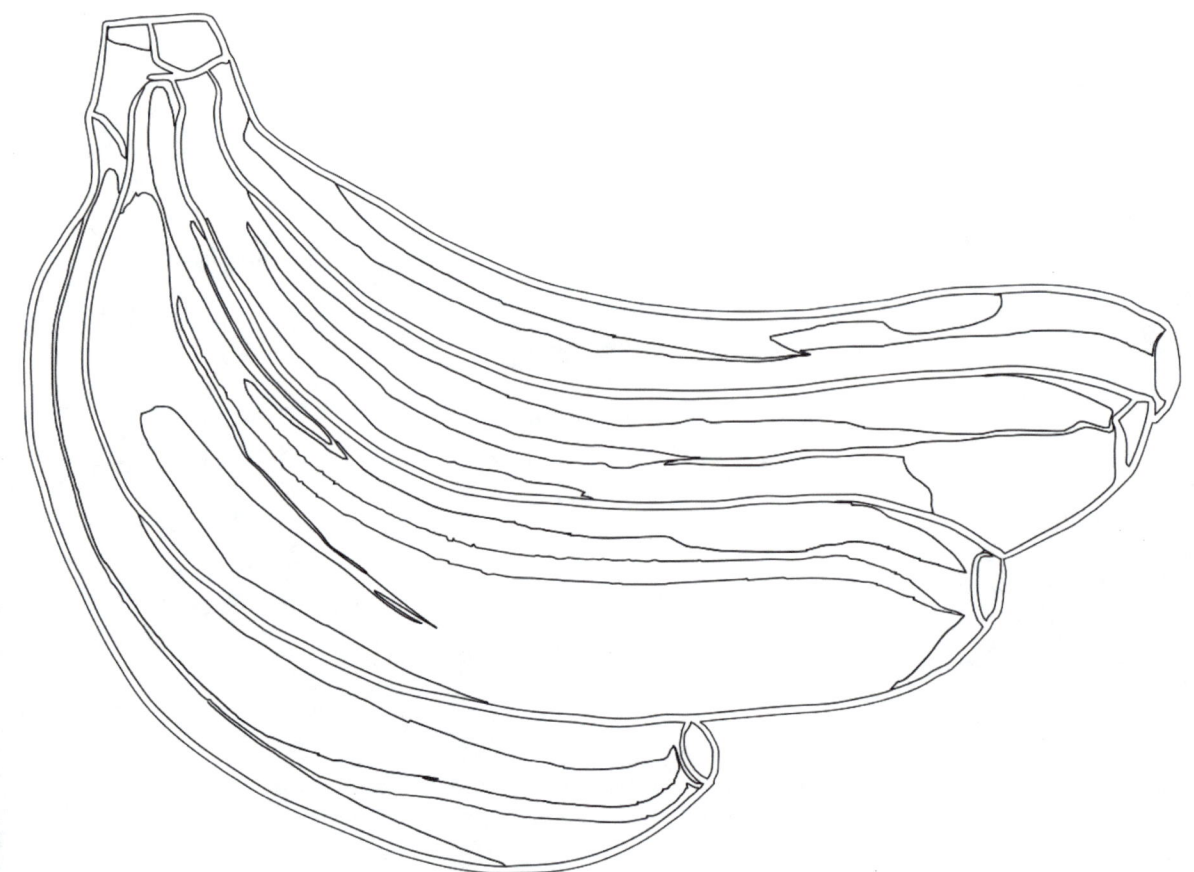

BANANA

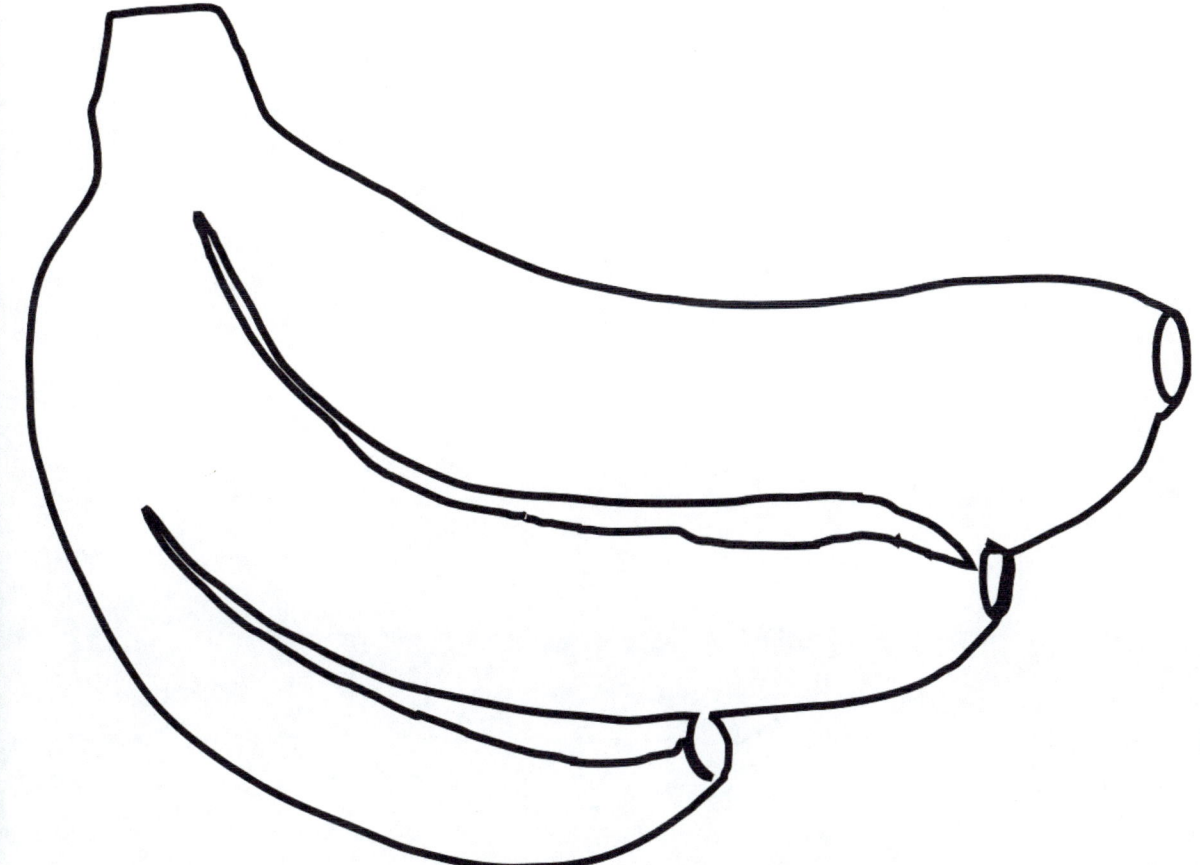

BANANA

ILLUSTRATE YOUR OWN BANANA ON THIS CANVAS

CANTALOUPE

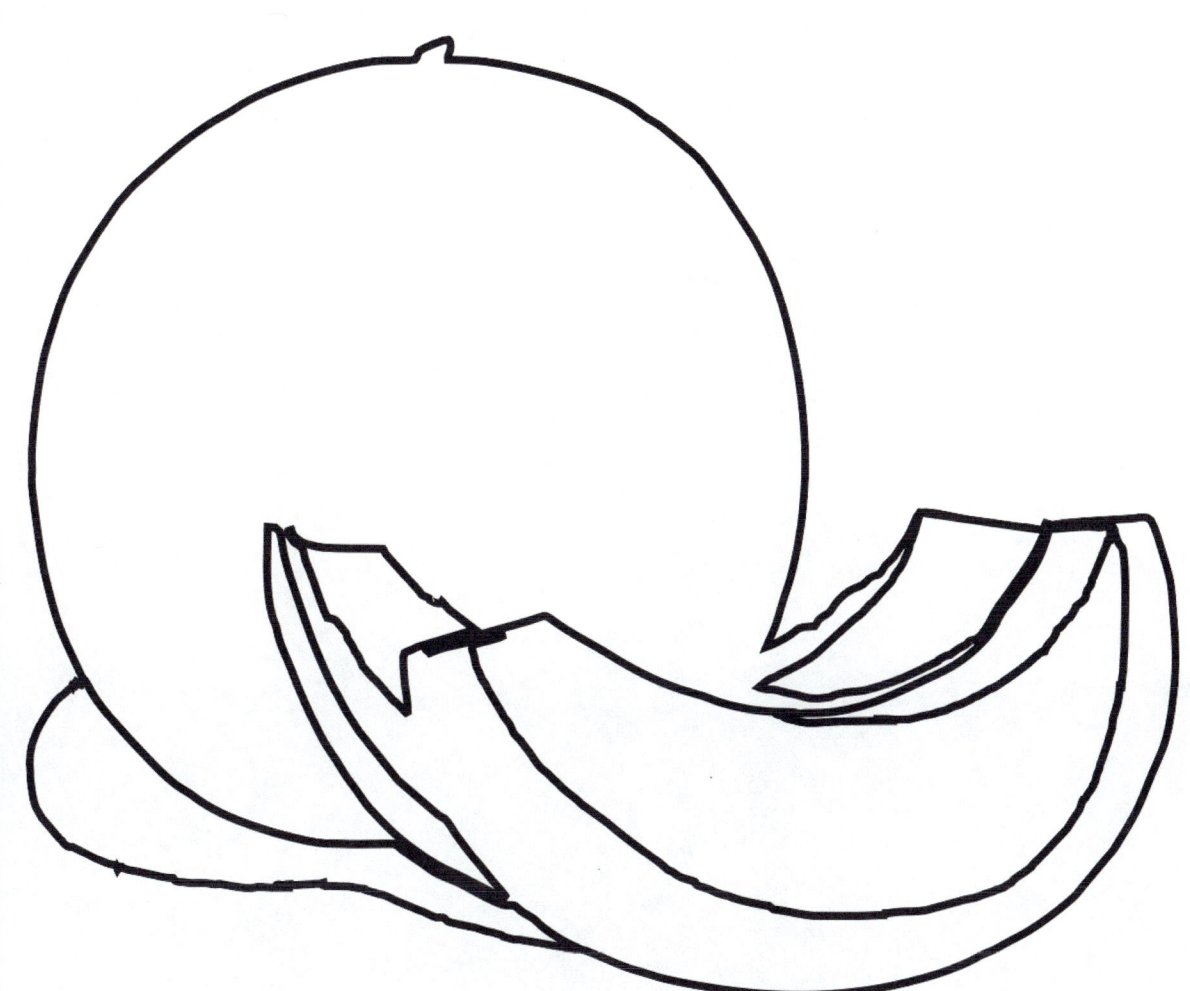

CANTALOUPE

ILLUSTRATE YOUR OWN CANTALOUPE ON THIS CANVAS

DATE

DATE

ILLUSTRATE YOUR OWN DATE ON THIS CANVAS

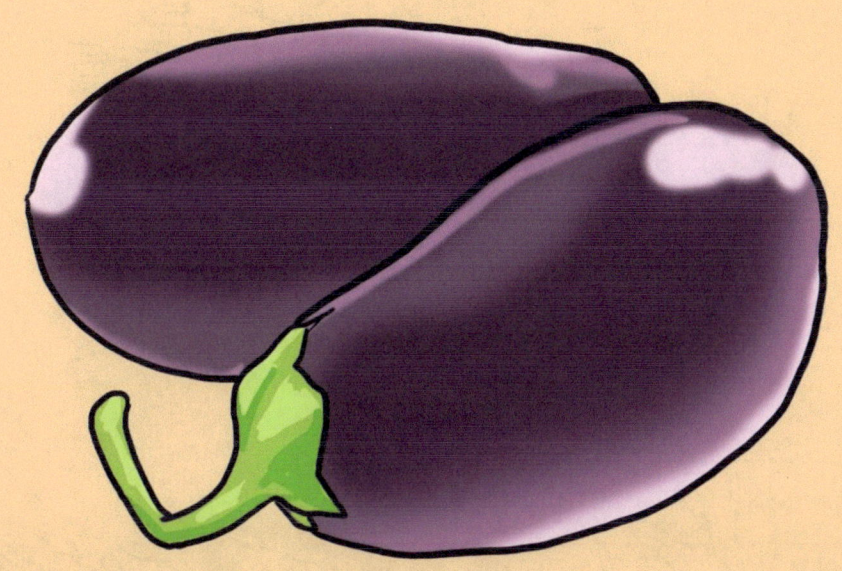

EGGPLANT

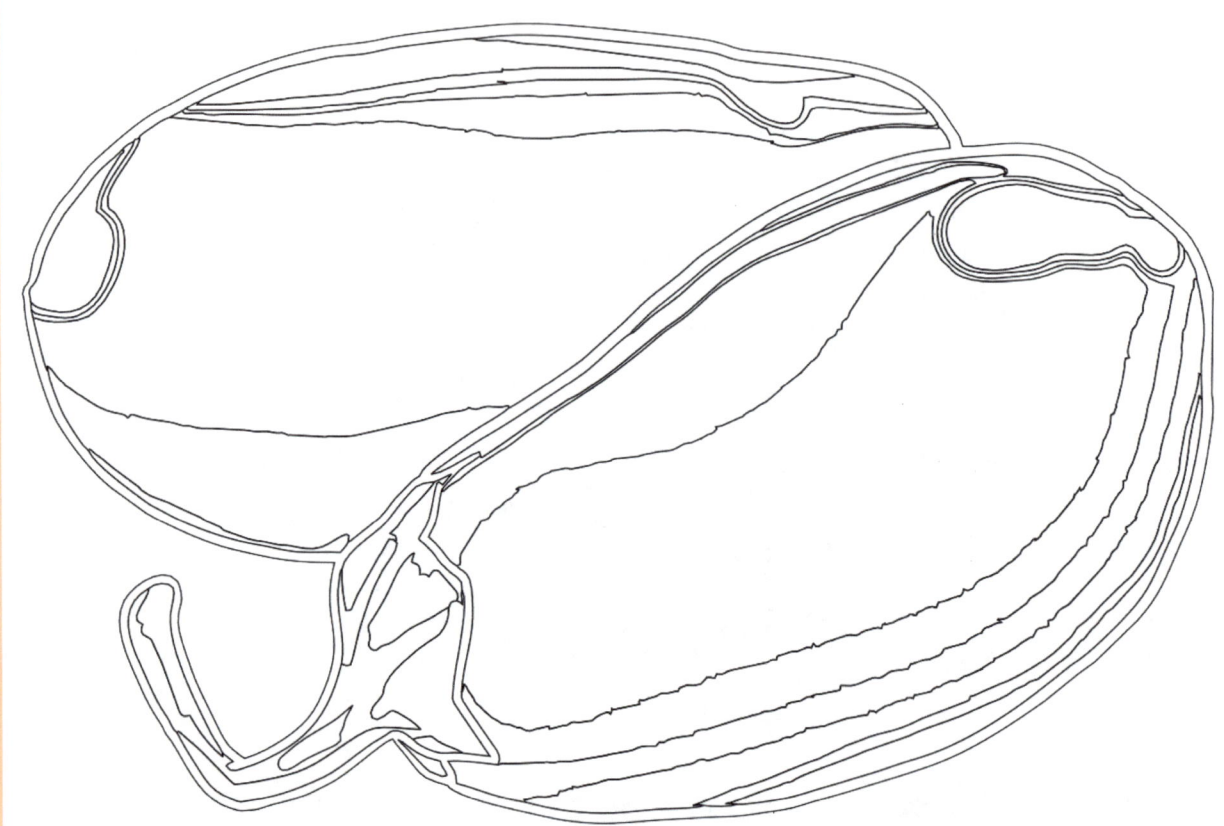

EGGPLANT

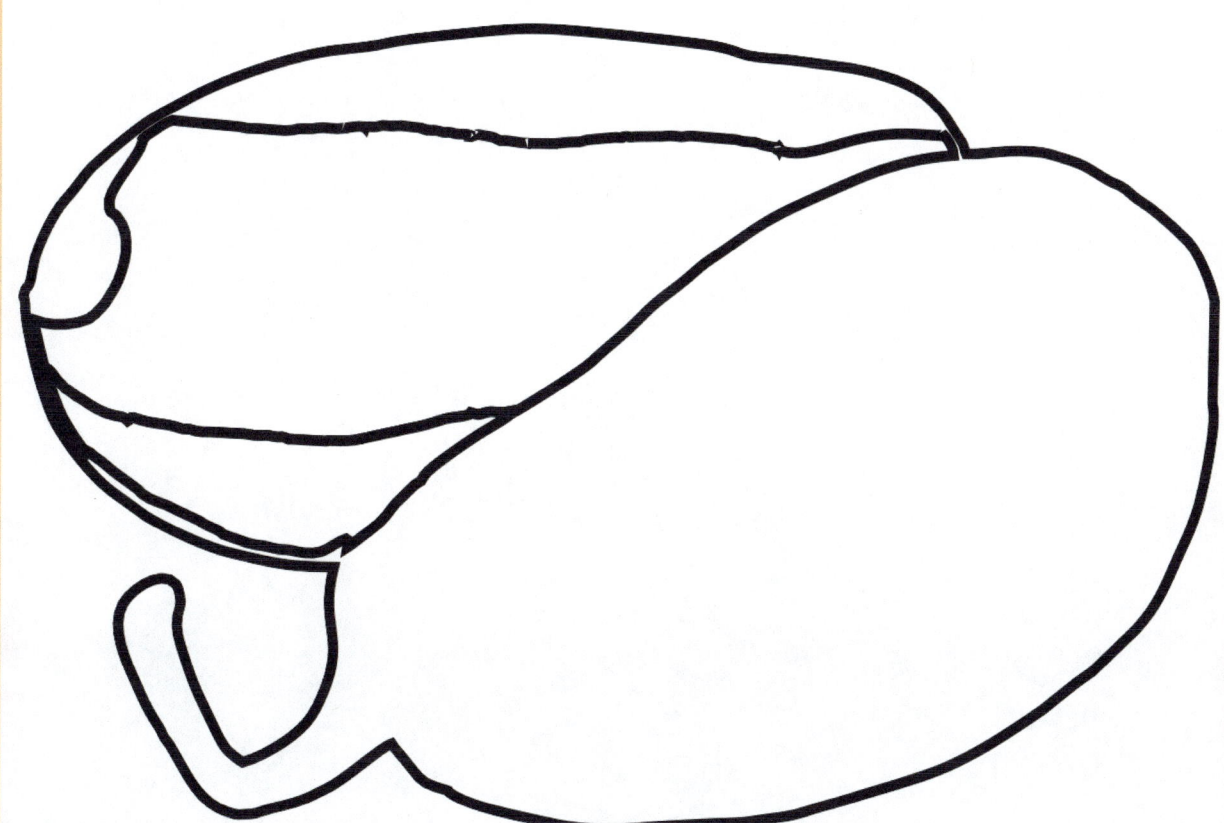

EGGPLANT

ILLUSTRATE YOUR OWN EGGPLANT ON THIS CANVAS

FIG

FIG

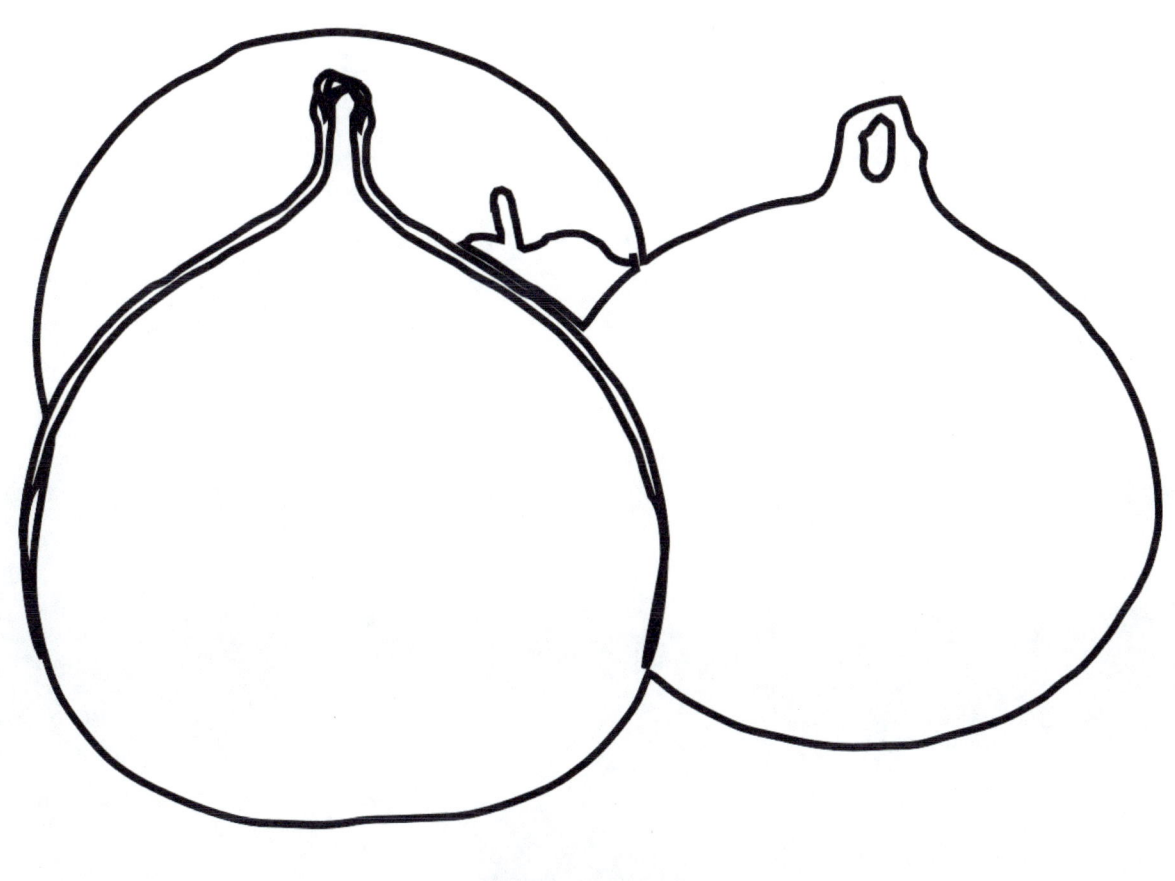

FIG

ILLUSTRATE YOUR OWN FIG ON THIS CANVAS

GOOSEBERRY

GOOSEBERRY

ILLUSTRATE YOUR OWN GOOSEBERRY ON THIS CANVAS

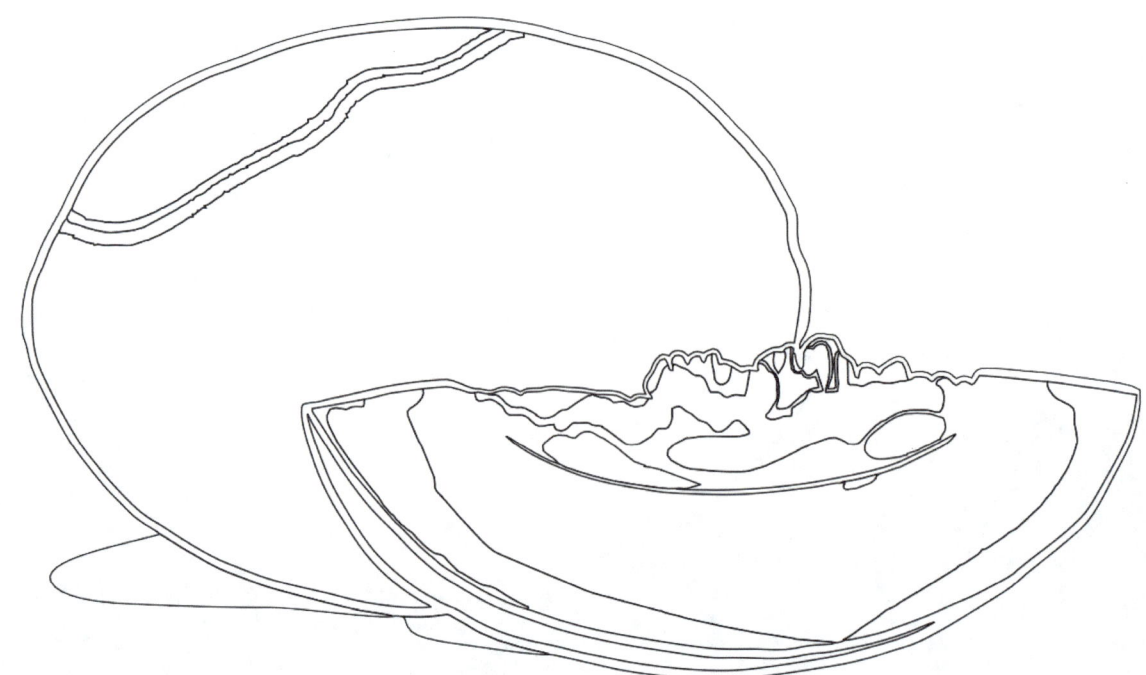

HONEYDEW

HONEYDEW

ILLUSTRATE YOUR OWN HONEYDEW ON THIS CANVAS

ITA PALM

ITA PALM

ITA PALM

ILLUSTRATE YOUR OWN ITA PALM ON THIS CANVAS

JUJUBE

JUJUBE

JUJUBE

ILLUSTRATE YOUR OWN JUJUBE ON THIS CANVAS

KIWI

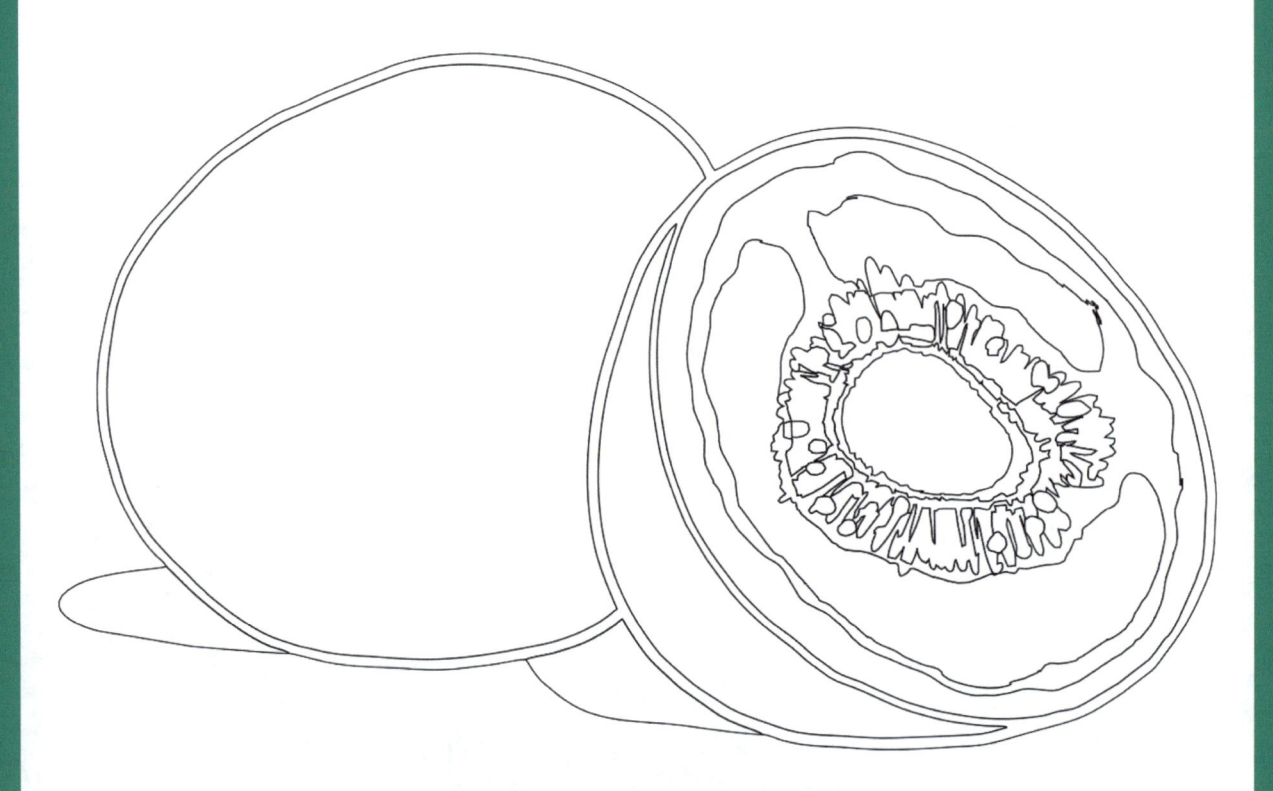

KIWI

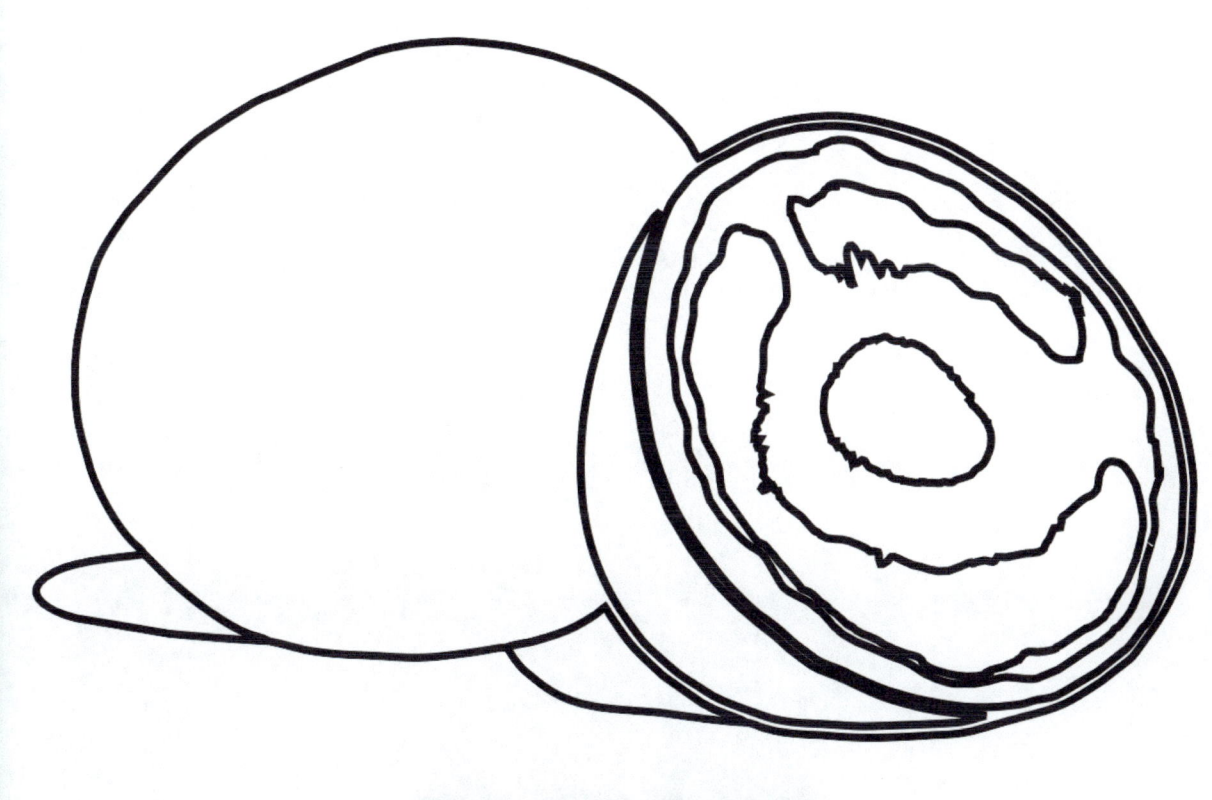

KIWI

ILLUSTRATE YOUR OWN KIWI ON THIS CANVAS

LEMON

LEMON

LEMON

ILLUSTRATE YOUR OWN LEMON ON THIS CANVAS

MANGO

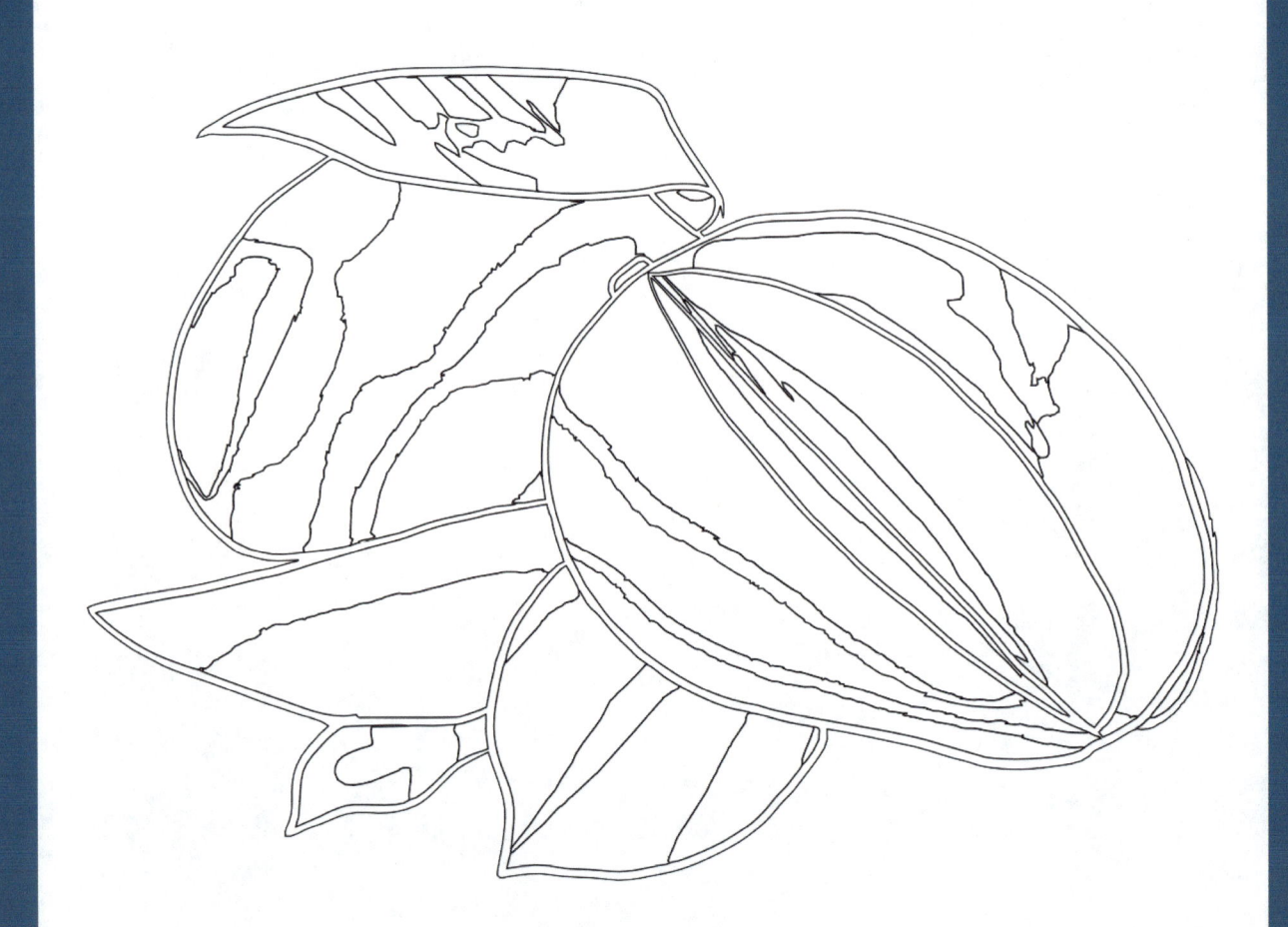

MANGO

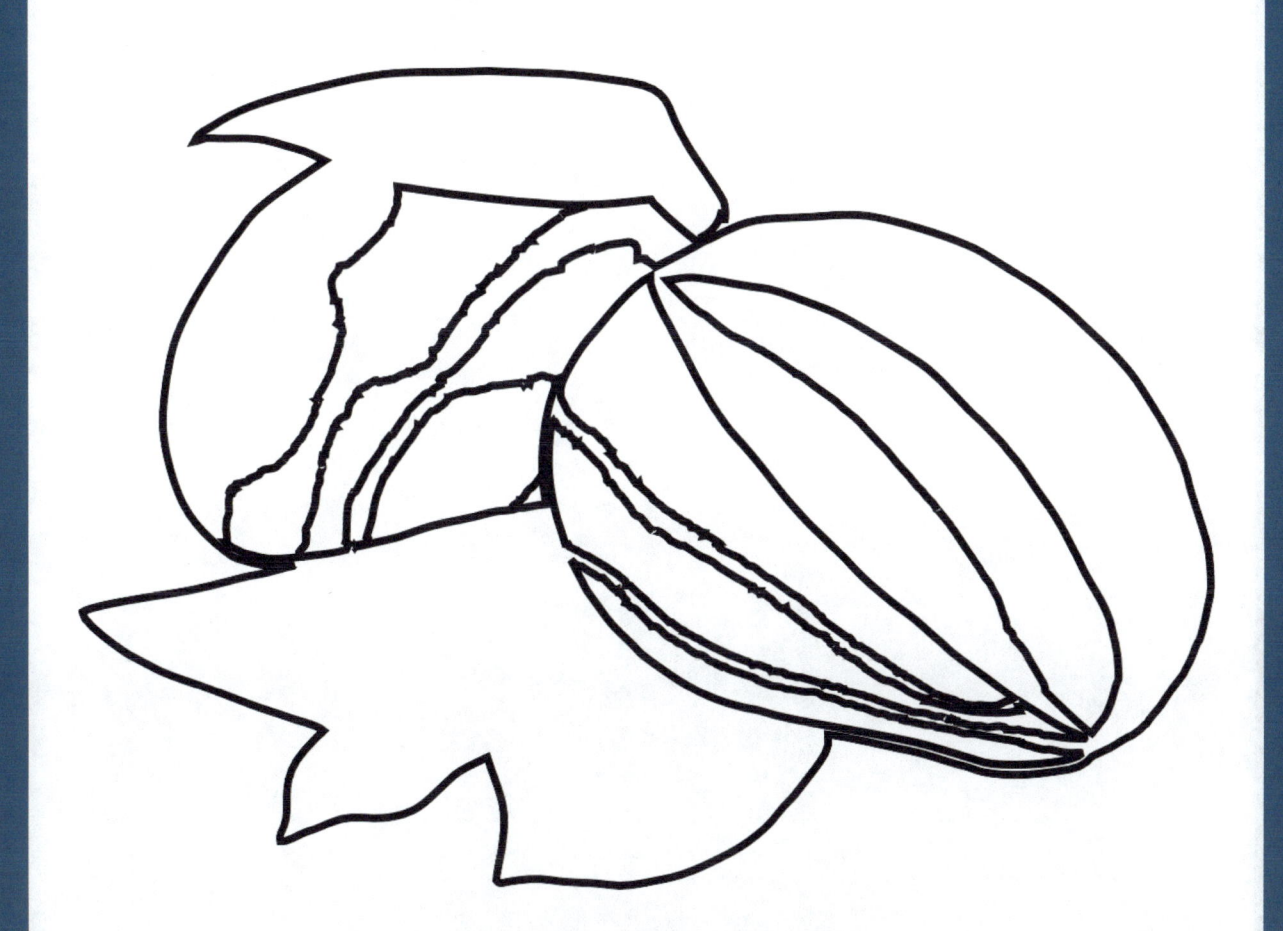

MANGO

ILLUSTRATE YOUR OWN MANGO ON THIS CANVAS

NECTARINE

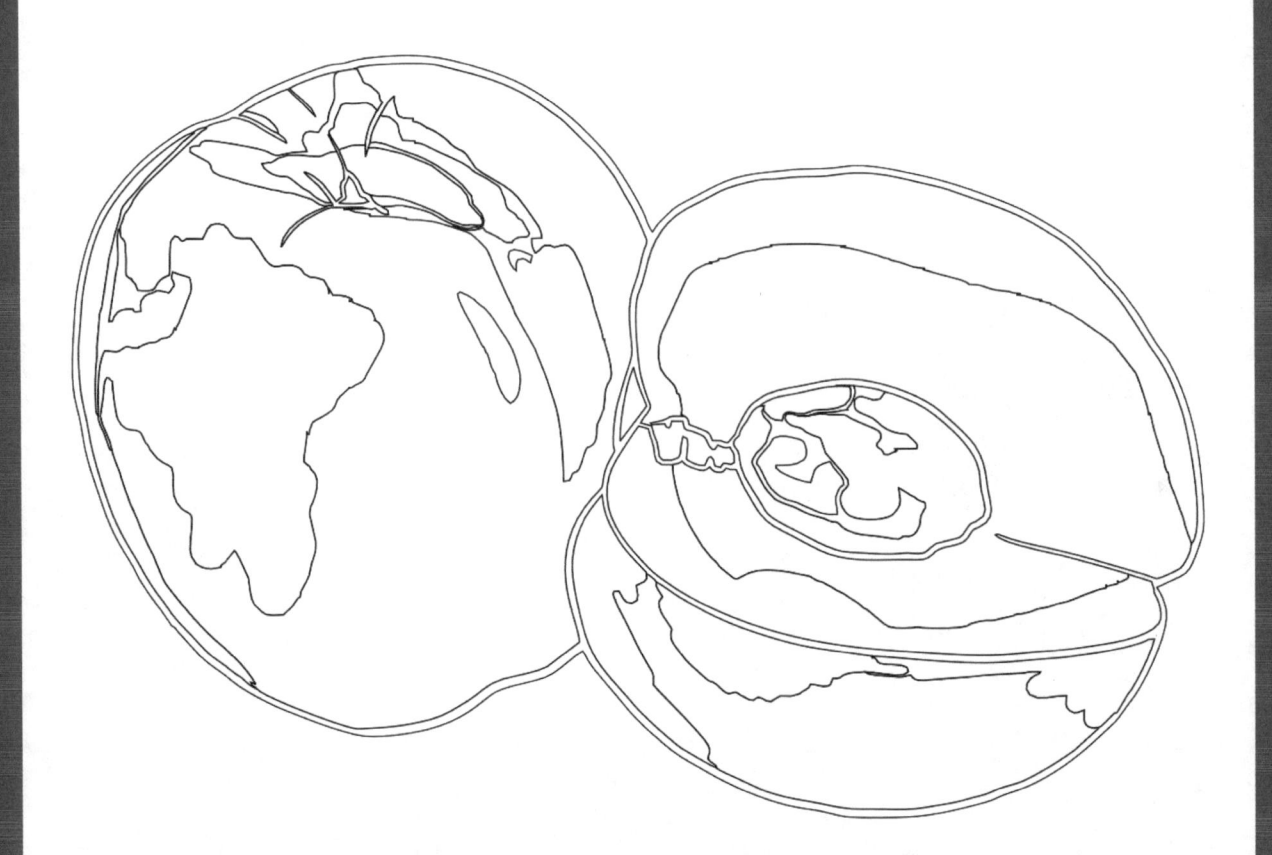

NECTARINE

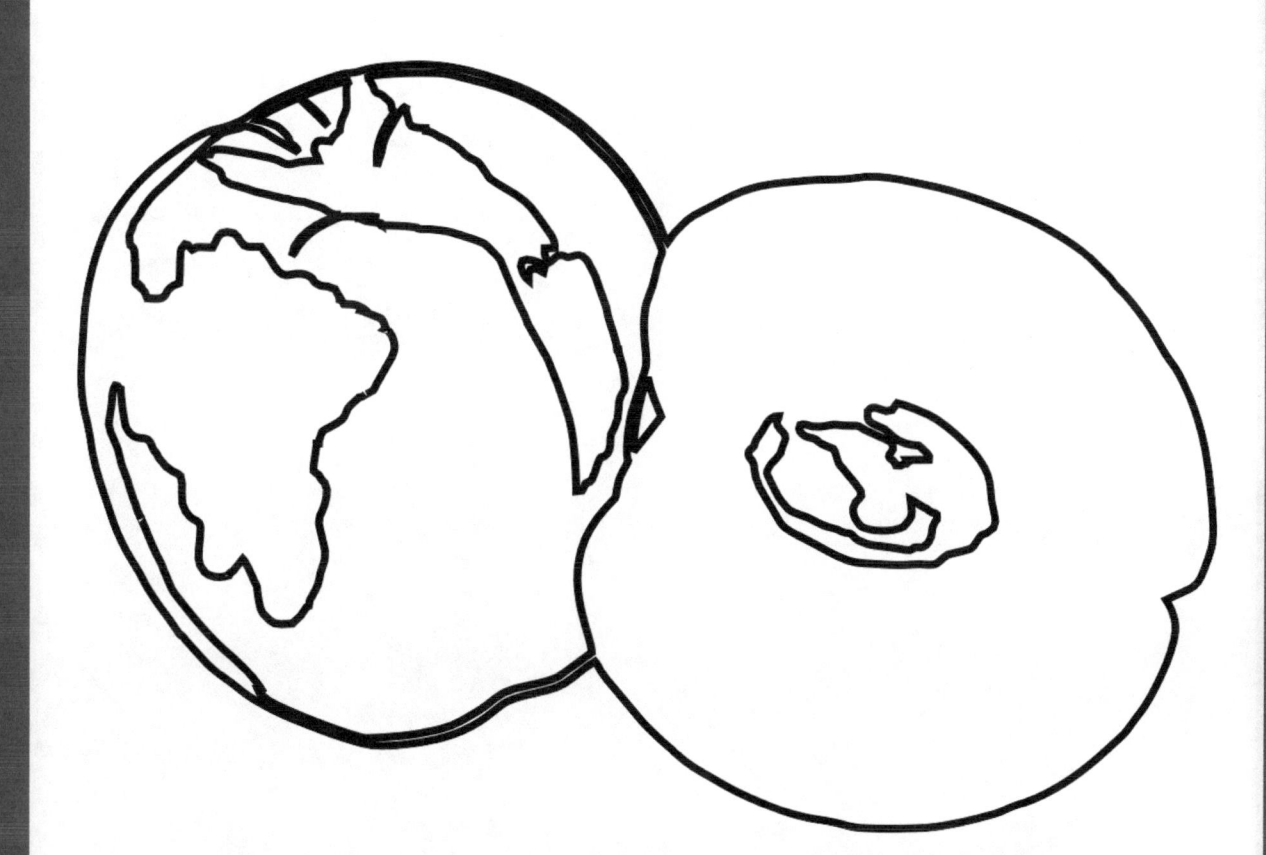

NECTARINE

ILLUSTRATE YOUR OWN NECTARINE ON THIS CANVAS

OLIVE

OLIVE

OLIVE

ILLUSTRATE YOUR OWN OLIVE ON THIS CANVAS

PAPAYA

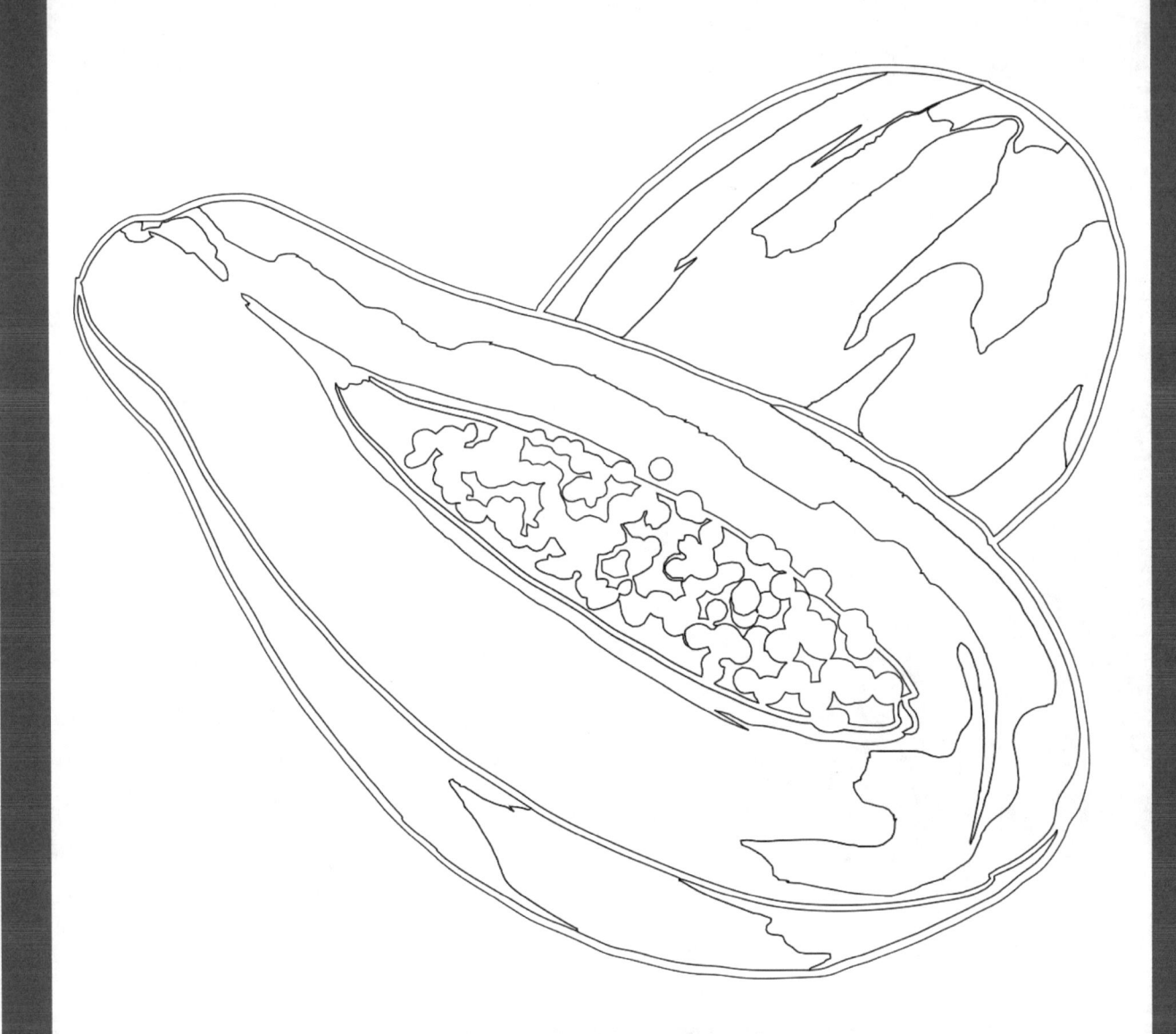

PAPAYA

PAPAYA

ILLUSTRATE YOUR OWN PAPAYA ON THIS CANVAS

QUINCE

QUINCE

QUINCE

ILLUSTRATE YOUR OWN QUINCE ON THIS CANVAS

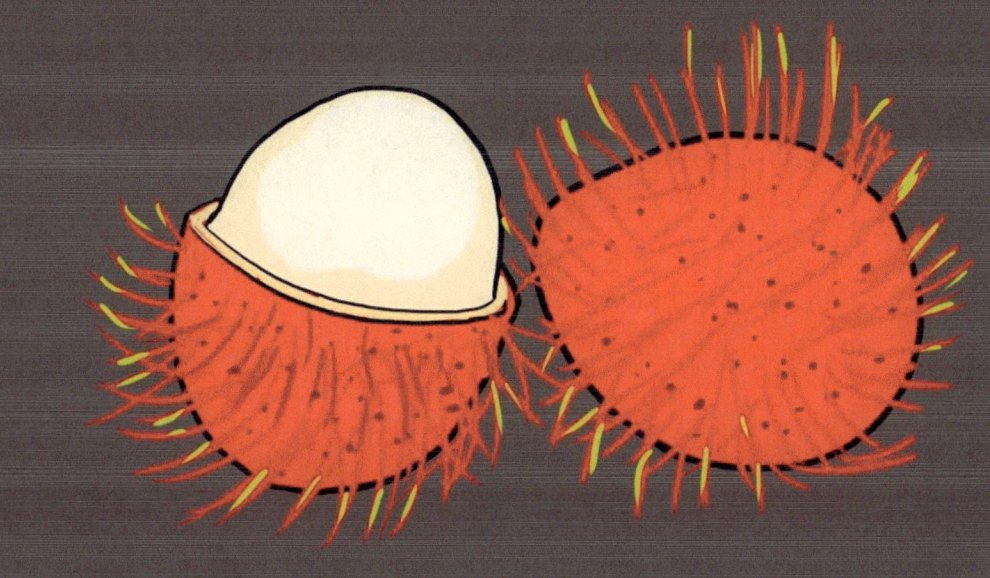

RAMBUTAN

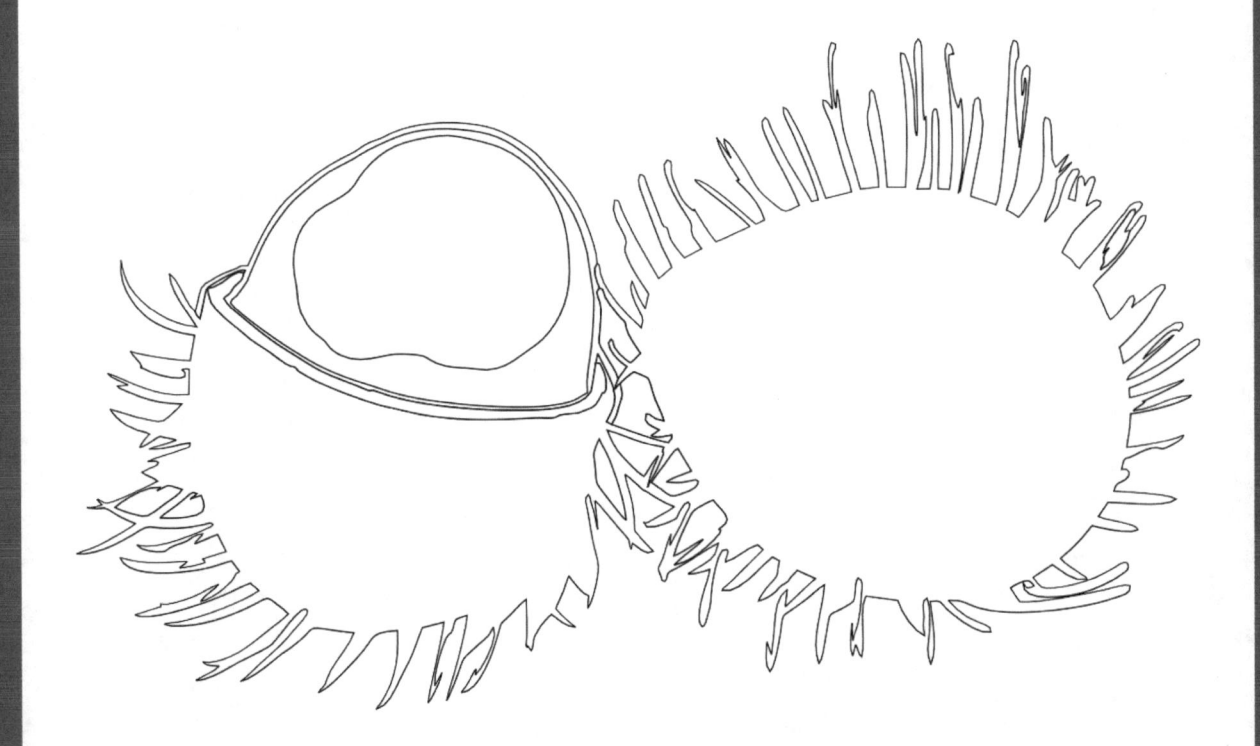

RAMBUTAN

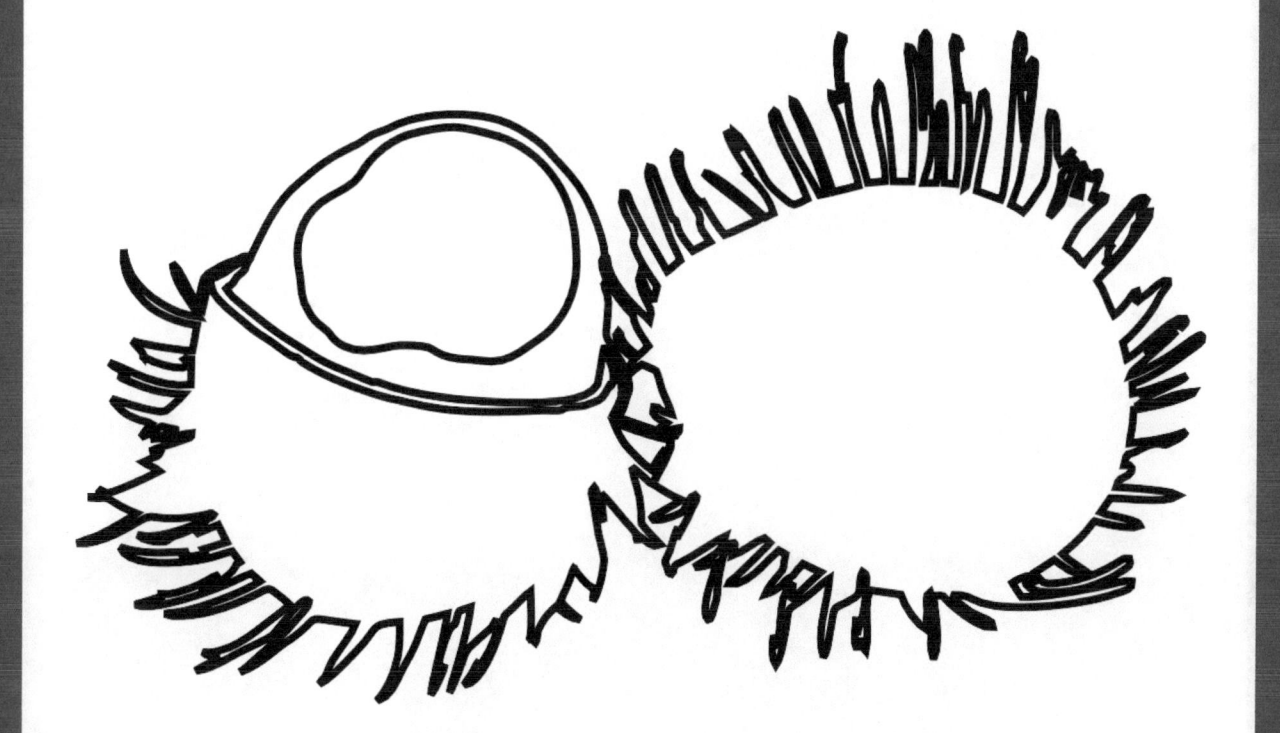

RAMBUTAN

ILLUSTRATE YOUR OWN RAMBUTAN ON THIS CANVAS

STAR FRUIT

STAR FRUIT

STAR FRUIT

ILLUSTRATE YOUR OWN STAR FRUIT ON THIS CANVAS

TANGELO

TANGELO

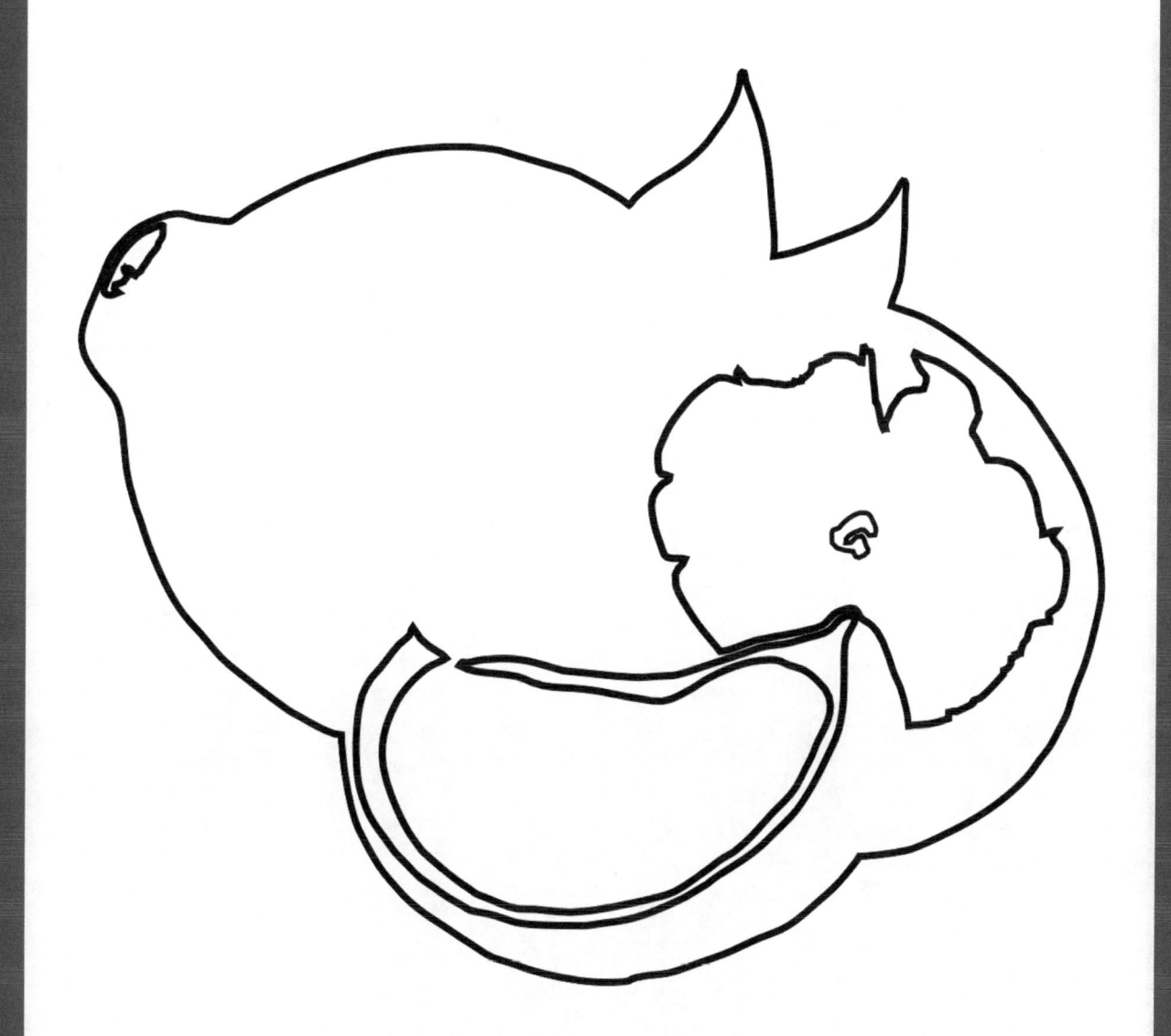

TANGELO

ILLUSTRATE YOUR OWN TANGELO ON THIS CANVAS

UGLI

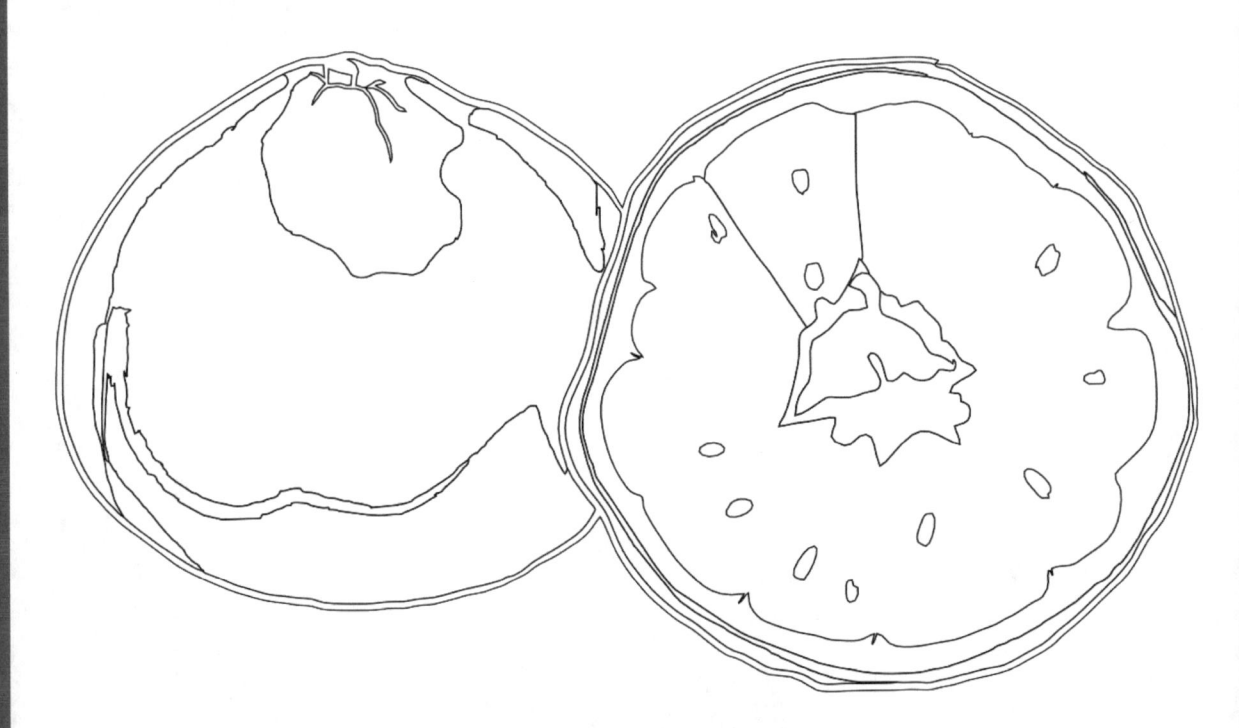

UGLI

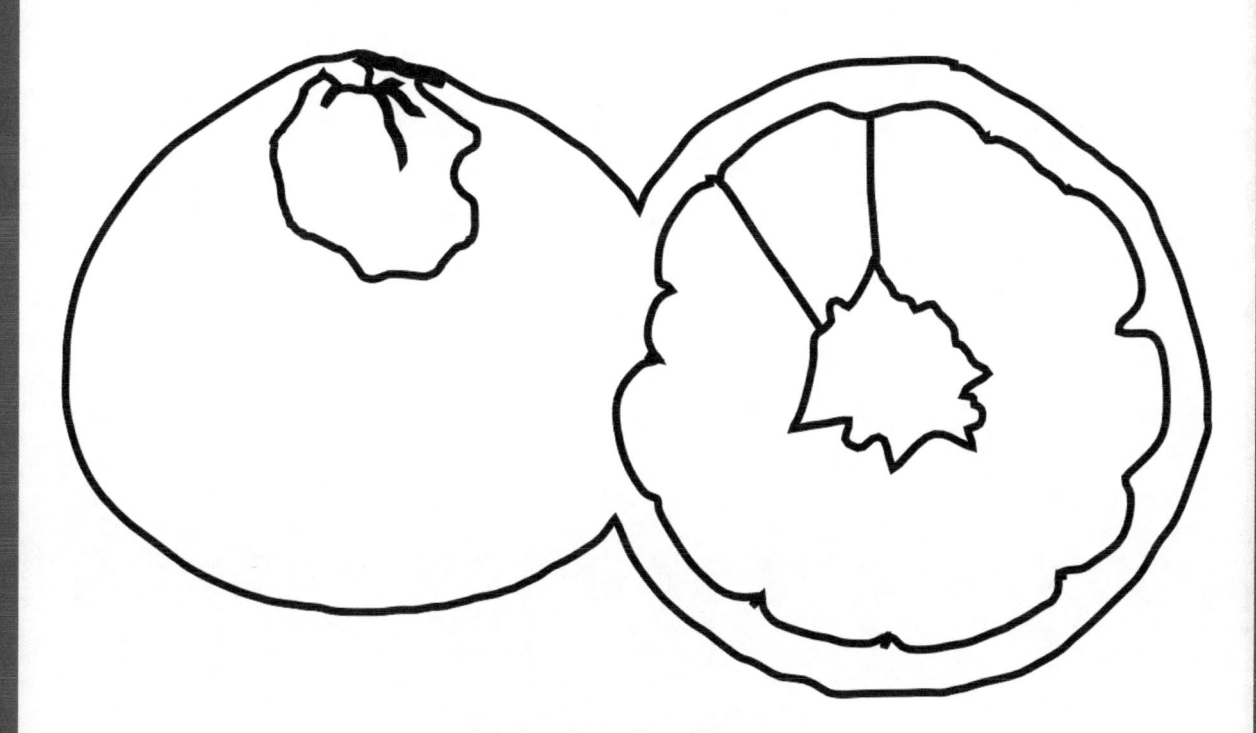

UGLI

ILLUSTRATE YOUR OWN UGLI ON THIS CANVAS

VOAVANGA

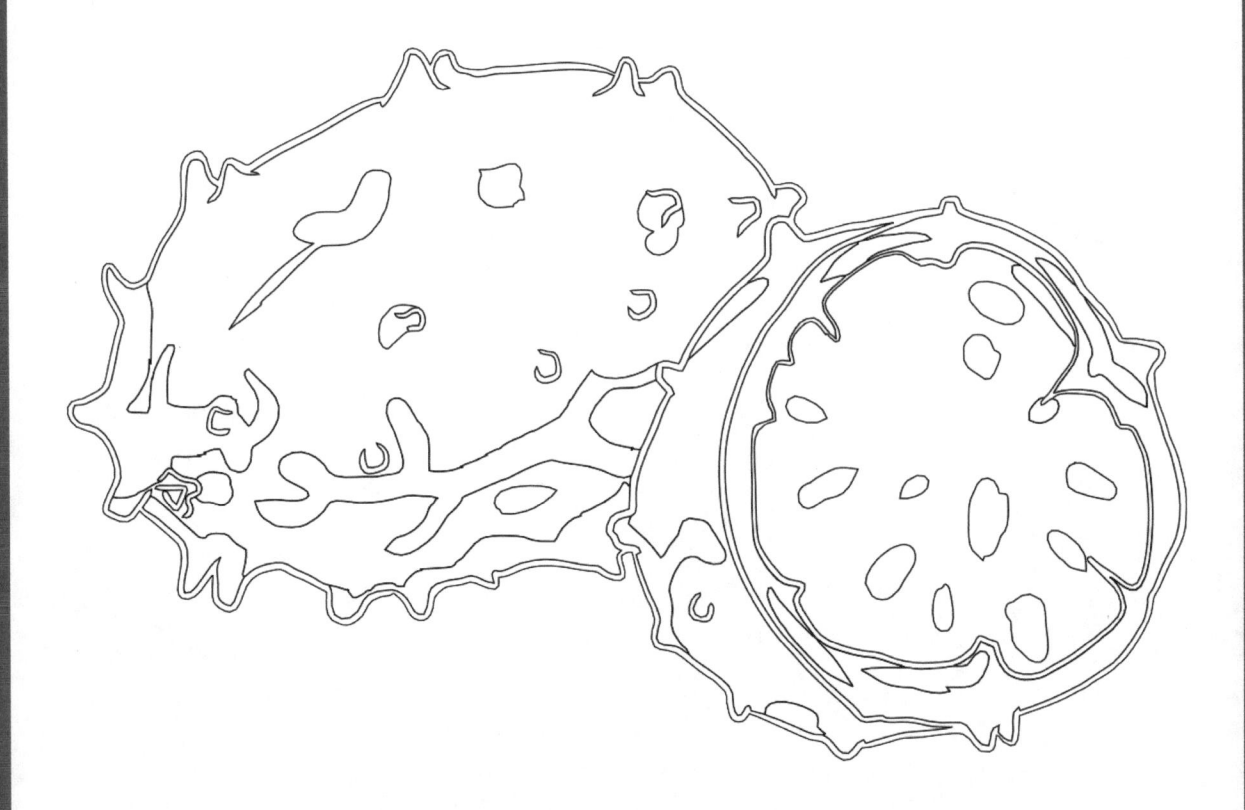

VOAVANGA

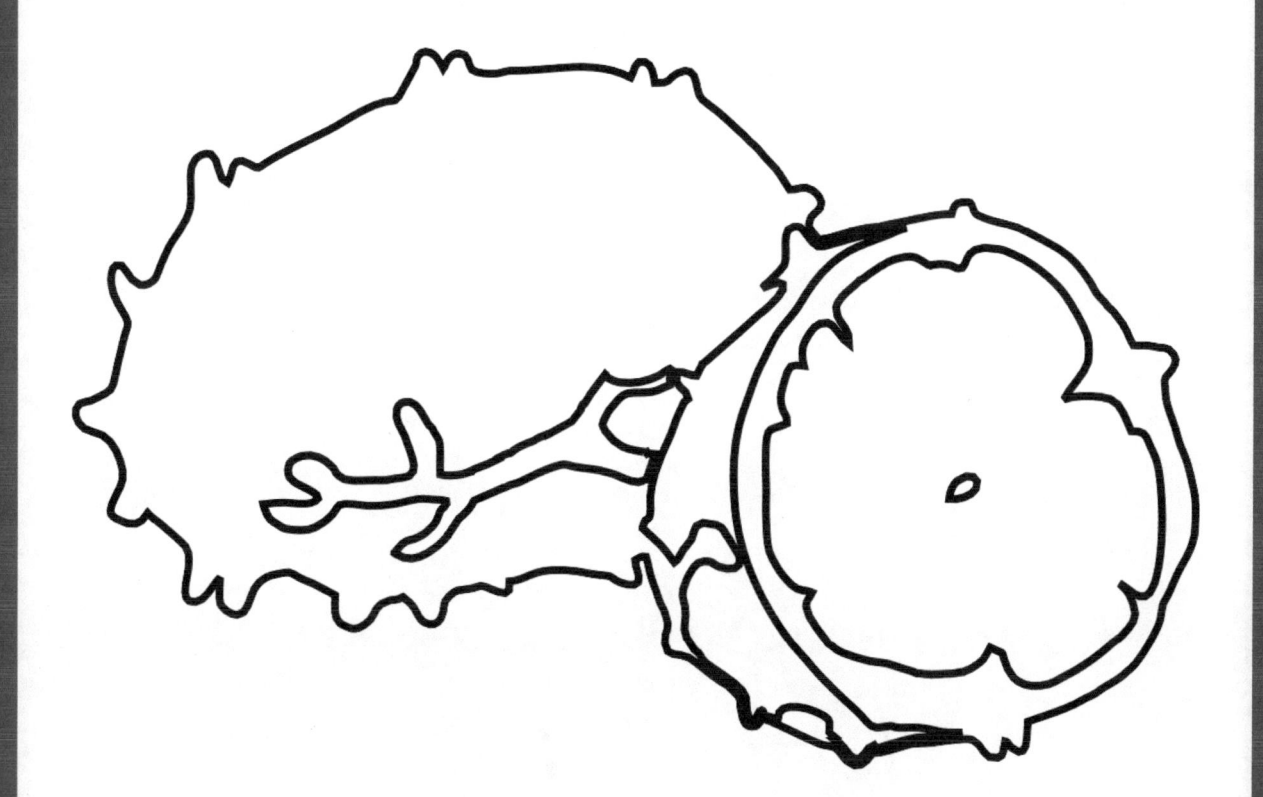

VOAVANGA

ILLUSTRATE YOUR OWN VOAVANGA ON THIS CANVAS

WATERMELON

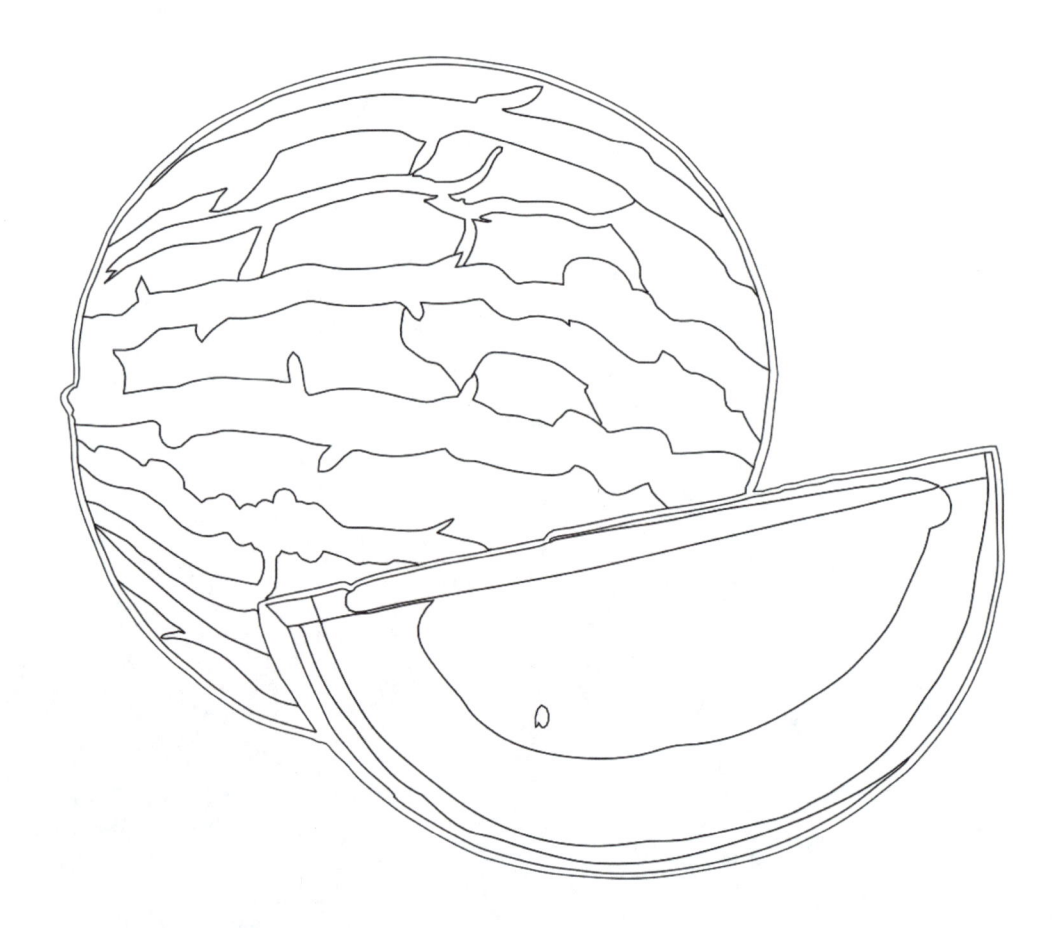

WATERMELON

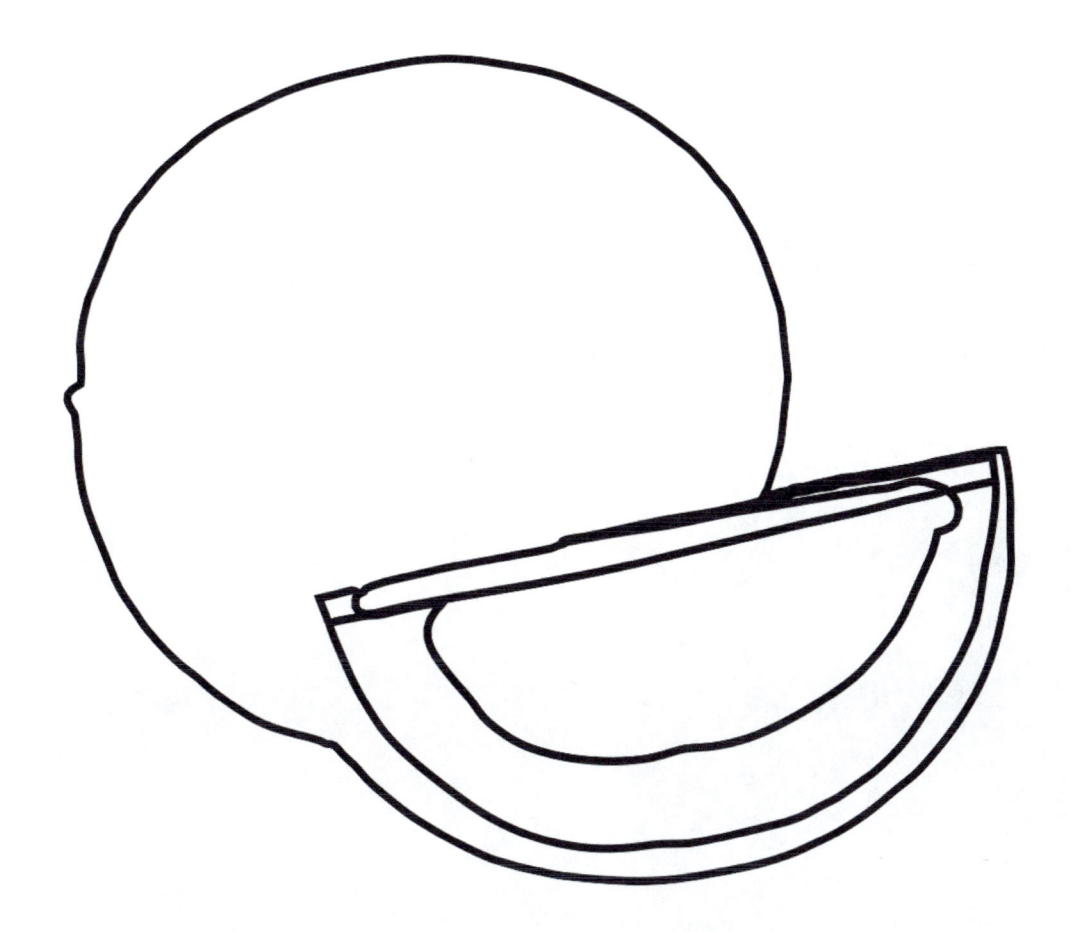

WATERMELON

ILLUSTRATE YOUR OWN WATERMELON ON THIS CANVAS

XIGUA

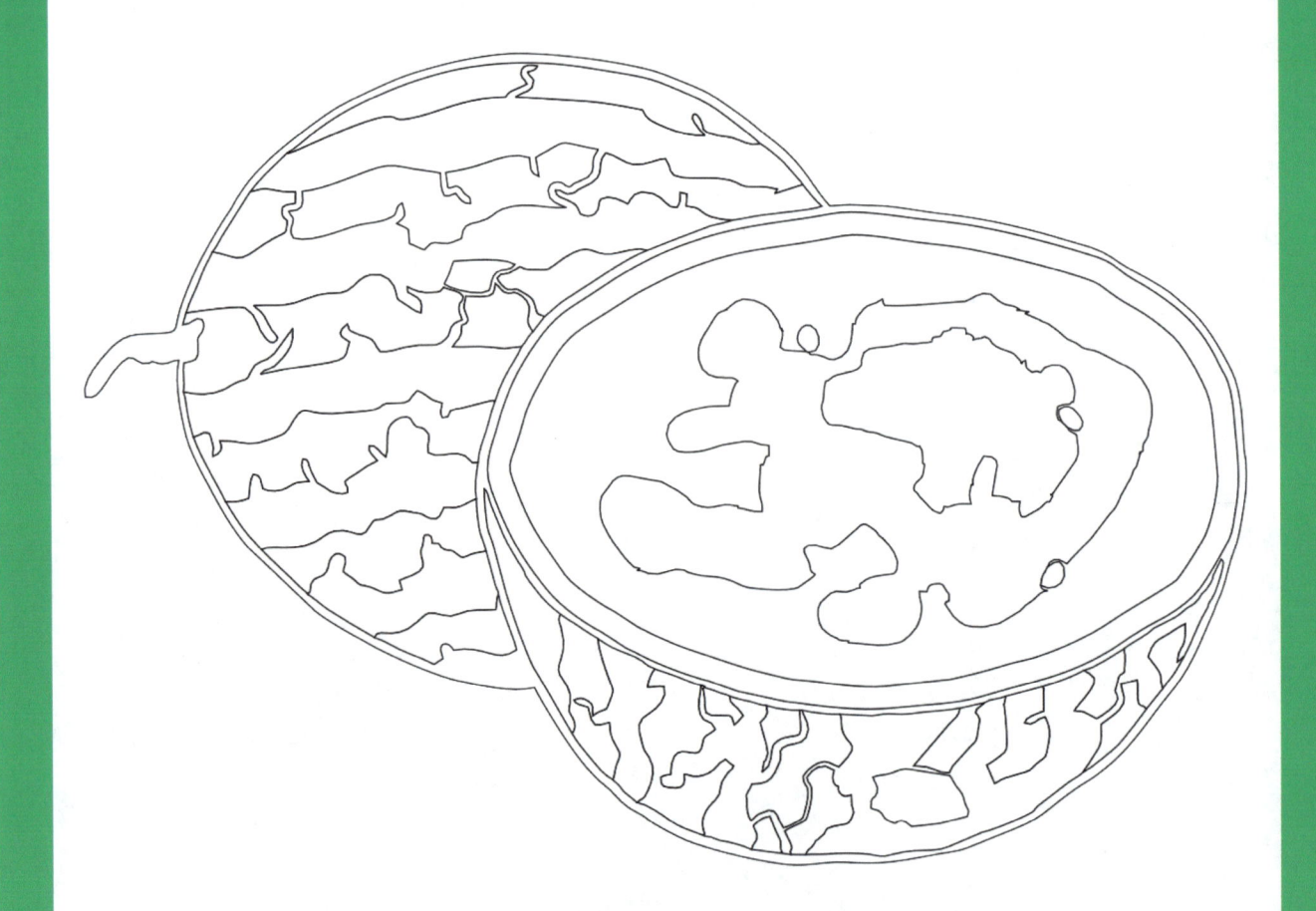

XIGUA

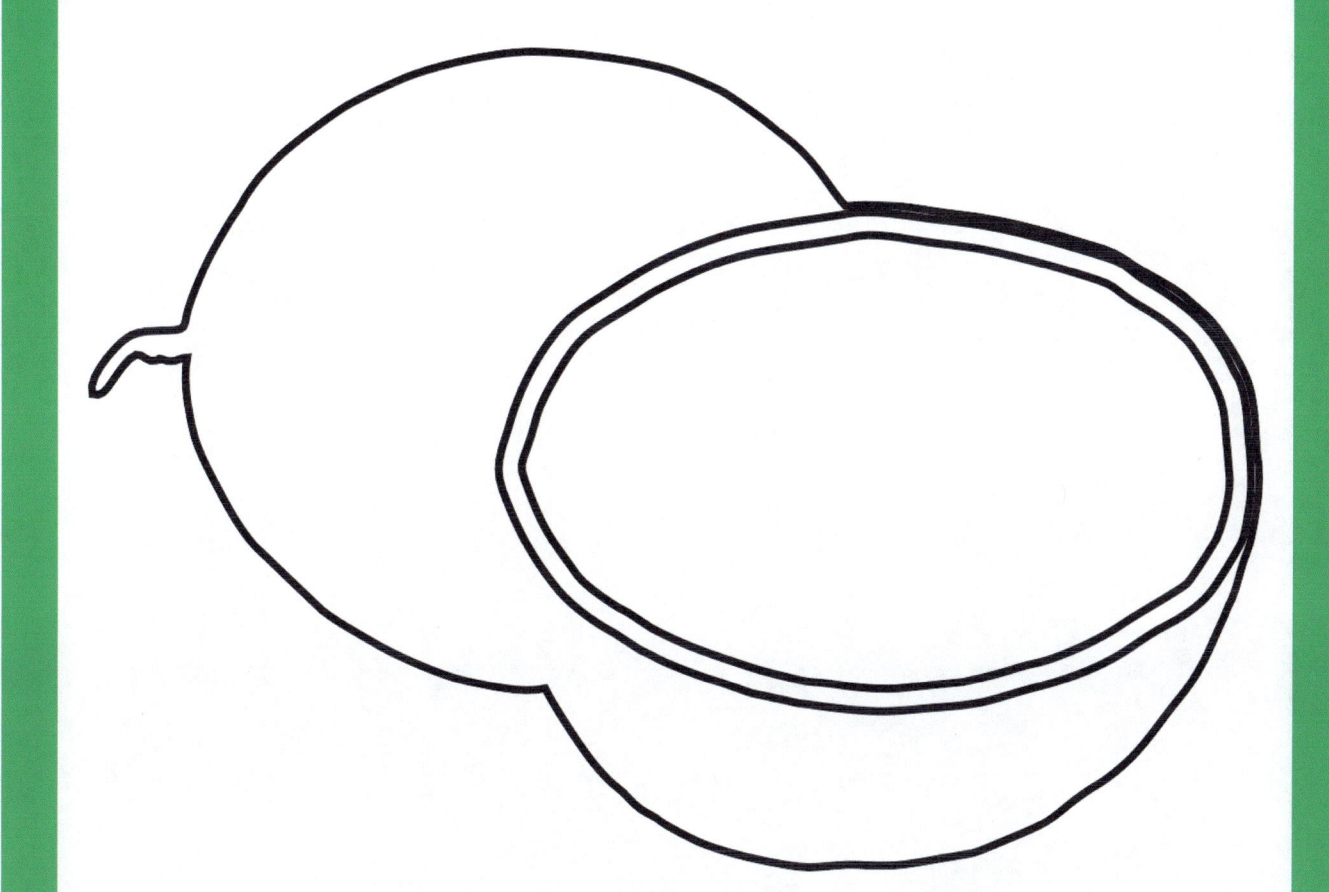

XIGUA

ILLUSTRATE YOUR OWN XIGUA ON THIS CANVAS

YUMBERRY

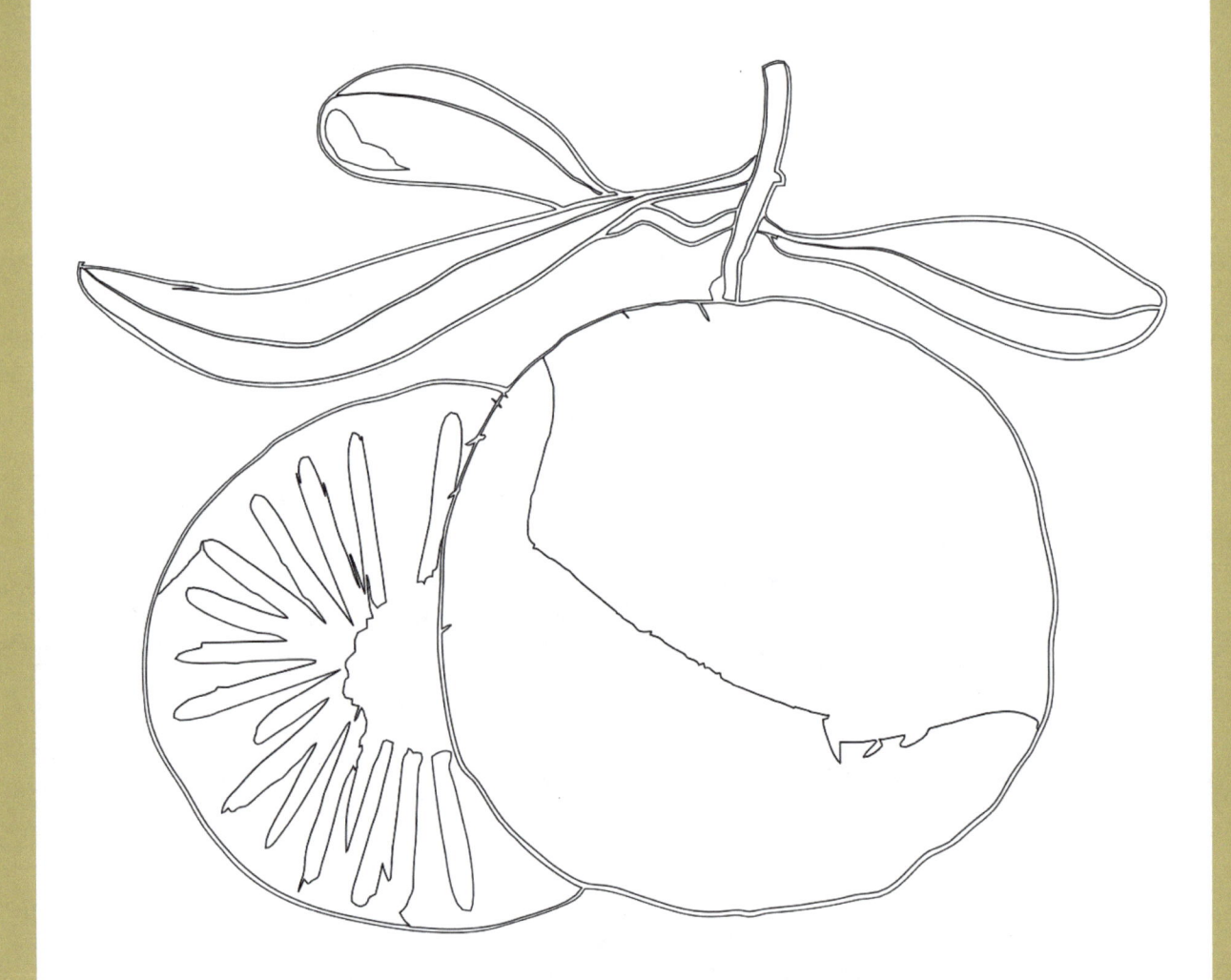

YUMBERRY

YUMBERRY

ILLUSTRATE YOUR OWN YUMBERRY ON THIS CANVAS

ZUCHINNI

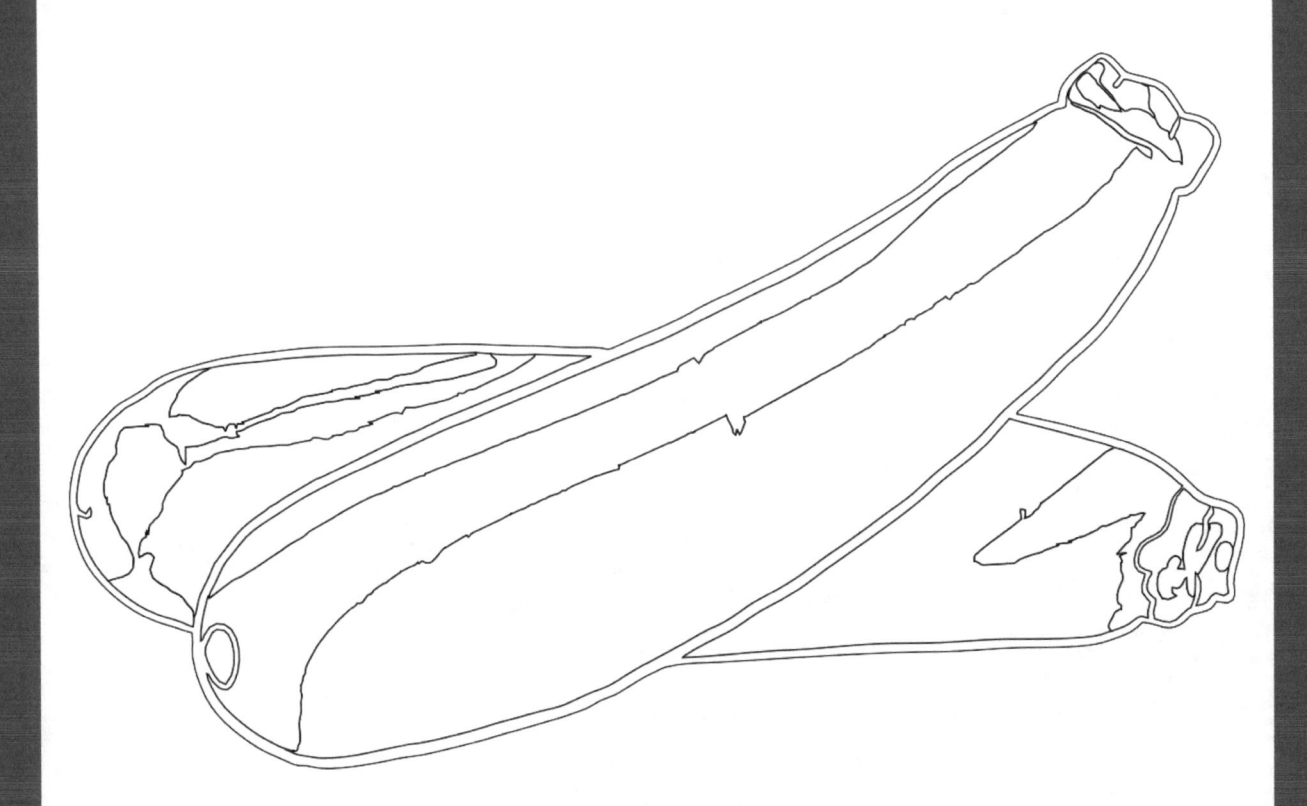

ZUCHINNI

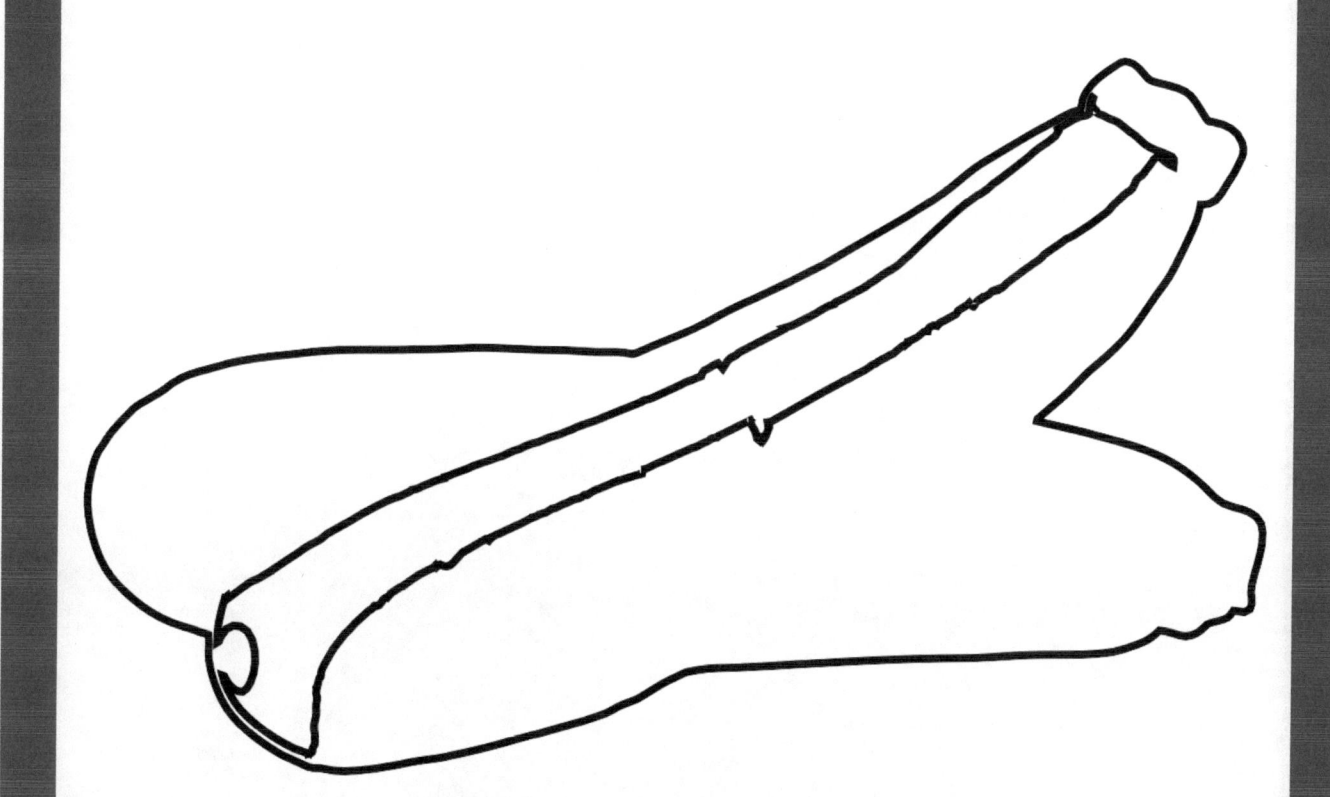

ZUCHINNI

ILLUSTRATE YOUR OWN ZUCHINNI ON THIS CANVAS

LIST THE COLORS YOU CHOSE TO USE FOR EACH FRUIT HERE.

APPLE –

BANANA –

CANTALOUPE –

DATE –

EGGPLANT –

FIG –

GOOSEBERRY –

HONEYDEW –

ITA PALM –

JUJUBE –

KIWI –

LEMON –

MANGO –

NECTARINE –

OLIVE –

PAPAYA –

QUINCE –

RAMBUTAN –

STAR FRUIT –

TANGELO –

UGLI –

VOAVANGA –

WATERMELON –

XIGUA –

YUMBERRY –

ZUCHINNI –

We extend our heartfelt appreciation for acquiring **Volume 1** of our **Awesome Fruits Coloring Book for Kids**.

Thank You.

Made in the USA
Columbia, SC
24 July 2024